GOLFING TRIFLES

GOLFING TRIFLES

Edited by

P.J.M

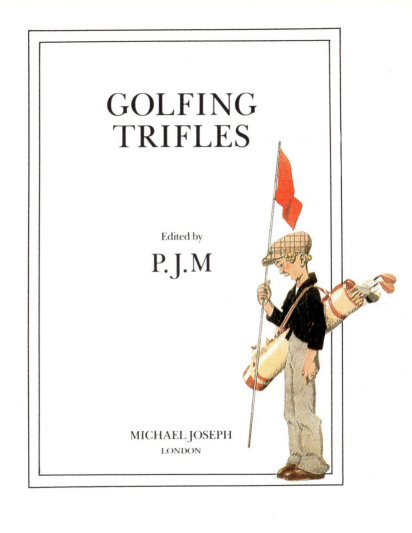

MICHAEL JOSEPH
LONDON

To Tony
Dominic and Katherine

First published in Great Britain by
Michael Joseph Limited
44 Bedford Square, London WC1
1985

© 1985 by P.J.M.

All Rights Reserved. No part of this publication
may be reproduced, stored in a retrieval system,
or transmitted in any form or by any means,
electronic, mechanical, photocopying, recording
or otherwise, without the prior permission of
the Copyright owner

British Library Cataloguing in Publication Data

P.J.M.
 Golfing trifles: a collection of poems and
 prose concerning the royal and ancient game.
 1. Golf — Anecdotes, facetiae, satire, etc.
 I. Title
 796.352   GV967

ISBN 0-7181-2568-1

Typesetting by Alacrity Phototypesetters,
Banwell Castle, Weston-super-Mare
Printed and bound in Italy by
Arnoldo Mondadori Co. Ltd.

From The Office	7
A Tee Spoon	9
Extracts from Club Records	10
The People In Front	13
Off My Game	17
The Golfiad	18
Love's Hazard	21
The Golfing Ghost	22
The Heart Of A Goof	25
The Wooden Putter	26
The Morning Round	29
The Golfer At Home	30
Duffers Yet	33
Seaside Golf	35
In Praise Of Golf	36
High Stakes	39
A Round With The Pro.	40
The Dreadful Hollow	43
After Tea	45
"Far And Sure!"	46
Acknowledgements	48

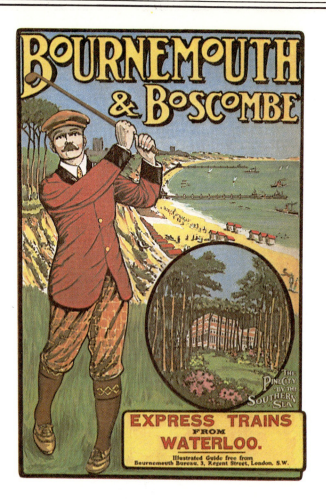

FROM THE OFFICE

My heart's on the golf-links,
  It's not here at all;
My heart's on the golf-links,
  Addressing the ball;
Addressing the wee ball,
  And following it through;
My heart's on the golf-links,
  Whatever I do.

              M.G.

A TEE SPOON

Oh, I would be the caddie-boy,
   Down at her feet to drop,
And build for her the sandy tee,
   And put the ball on top.

And I would be the driver slim,
   Around her still to swing,
E'en though my head should never reach
   The centre of that ring.

And I would be the tiny sphere,
   To thrill 'neath her address;
Not the wide atmo*sphere* itself
   Would hold such happiness.

And I would be the shaven green
   (No metaphor is meant);
She would approach, to find in me
   The (w)hole of her intent.

Ah, club! ah, ball! ah, senseless things!
   Might I so favoured be,
To her I would the question put(t),
   And she should make *my* tea.

                        E. M. Griffiths

EXTRACTS FROM CLUB RECORD BOOKS

Golf House, Jan. 19, 1782.

That Port and Punch shall be the ordinary Drink of the Society unless upon these days when the SILVER CLUB and CUPS are played for. At those Meetings Claret or any other Liquor more agreeable will be permitted.

ALEX DUNCAN, *Captain.*
THE HONOURABLE THE EDINBURGH
COMPANY OF GOLFERS

Golf House, Nov. 22, 1783.

The Company having collected a small sum for David Lindsay, an old ball-maker and caddie, now very old and infirm, being above 80 years of age, It was agreed that he should have one half-crown weekly during pleasure out of the Funds — to commence next Saturday.

WILL. INGLIS.
THE HONOURABLE THE EDINBURGH
COMPANY OF GOLFERS

DINNER BILL

Golf House, Leith, August 29, 1801

Dinner	£2	0	0
Bread and Biscuit	0	2	0
Porter, Ale, and Spruce	0	8	0
Gin and Brandy	0	6	8
Port and Sherry (7 bottles)	1	13	6
Claret (16 bottles)	5	12	0
Tody, Glasses, Wax Lights, and Servants	0	11	2
	£10	13	4

St. Andrews, 4th September 1779.

It is enacted that whoever shall be Captain of the Golf, and does not attend all the meetings to be appointed throughout the year, shall pay Two Pints of Claret for each meeting he shall be absent at, — to be drunk at such meeting; but this regulation is not to take place if the Captain be not in Fife at the time.

WALTER BOSWELL.
THE ROYAL AND ANCIENT
GOLF CLUB OF ST. ANDREWS

St. Andrews, 4th August 1780.

The Society took into their consideration that their Golfing Jackets are in bad condition, — Have agreed that they shall have new ones — viz. Red with yellow buttons. The undermentioned gentlemen have likewise agreed to have an Uniform Frock — viz. a Buff colour with a Red Cap. The Coat to be half lapelled, the Button white.

BALCARRES, *and Ten others.*
THE ROYAL AND ANCIENT
GOLF CLUB OF ST. ANDREWS

Bruntsfield Links, 24th June 1815.

No particular business occurred at this meeting, but as the news had that morning arrived of the entry of the Allies into Paris, it put the whole Members into such spirits that the glass circulated pretty freely, and the usual hour of departure was protracted to the detriment of the stock. Bill, £4:8:6; whereof from stock, £2:0:6.

ROBT. STODART.
BRUNTSFIELD LINKS GOLF CLUB

Bruntsfield Links, 1st July 1774.

The meeting was of opinion that a Boy should be made choice of and engaged to call on each member every Saturday morning, and take the names of those who propose dining on that day, and that he shall serve as waiter in time of dinner, and also attend the Preses on the Saturdays, as a caddie for carrying his clubs. They also agreed that a suit of cloaths be immediately furnished, to be worn by him on Saturdays and Sundays only. In consideration of his trouble he is to be paid Six shillings per quarter from the funds of the Society.

EDINBURGH BURGESS GOLFING SOCIETY

Bruntsfield Links, 9th April 1784.

The Society authorise the Treasurer to pay the officer the price of a pair of shoes on account of the late increase of members, which occasioned a great deal of additional walking to him.

EDINBURGH BURGESS GOLFING SOCIETY

from
THE PEOPLE IN FRONT

HAZLITT thought it one of the best things in life to be known only as "the gentle-man in the parlour," and certainly it is a pleasant title. There is something so respectable about its anonymity, and yet it suggests all the romance of wayfaring. Other titles formed on somewhat similar lines suggest nothing but feelings of hatred and contempt. Such is that of the large class of golfers whom we call simply "the people in front." When the clocks have been put back and darkness falls prematurely on the links, they are more than ever detestable.

It is true that they are not, as a rule, in the least to blame for the delay; so much we grudgingly admit, but it does not make their little ways the less irritating. They waggle for hours; they stroll rather than walk; they dive into their monstrous bags in search of the right club and then it is the wrong number, but they are not sorry that we have been troubled; their putting is a kind of funereal ping-pong. We could forgive them all these tricks, if it were not for the absurd punctilio with which they observe the rules. They will insist on waiting for the people in front of them when it must be palpable even to their intellects that the best shot they ever hit in their lives would be fifty yards short.

Generally, as was said before, the people in front are not the real culprits. "I know it's not their fault," we say in the tone of the man who, as he broke his putter across his knee, exclaimed, "I know it's only a d — d game." That being so, it ought to make no difference to us who are the people for whom we have to wait. We should go no faster and no slower if Bobby Jones and Harry Vardon were playing in front of us instead of that old lady who scoops the ball along with a club that goes up so obviously faster than it can ever come down. I suppose we must be golfing snobs, because it does make a great difference. To be kept waiting by the eminent (I mean the eminent in golf) is to be reconciled to the

inevitability of things, whereas we always believe that the scooping lady could get along faster if she tried. Moreover, there is the disquieting hope that she may lose her ball. It would be of no real help to us if she did, but instinct is too strong for us. Every time her ball is seen heading for a gorse bush our heartfelt prayers go with it, and though attainment will swiftly prove disenchanting, it is a great moment when at last she waves us on and we stampede courteously past.

It is at that precise moment that we are most likely to hit our own ball into a gorse bush, for it is a law of nature that everybody plays a hole badly when going through. To be there and then repassed is one of the bitterest humiliations that golf can bring. But, of course, no rational being will endure it; for rather would we surrender the hole and make a rapid though undignified rush towards the next teeing ground. By this time, it is true, we are hot, flustered, and angry, and wish that the woman had kept her ball on the course.

My original list by no means exhausted the crimes that can be committed by the people in front. They can call us on and then, finding their ball in the nick of time, go on themselves, but that is an offence so black and repulsive that I cannot write about it. They can try over again the putt they have just missed, and this crime has become more fashionable since we have been taught to admire American assiduity in the practising of putts. They can take out a horrid little card and pencil, and, immobile in the middle of the green, write down their horrid little score. In that case, however, there is compensation, for there is no law of God or man that can prevent us from letting out a blaring yell of "Fore!" To see them duck and cower beneath the imaginary assault may not be much, but it is something. They may think us ill-mannered, but what does that matter? The worst they can do is to write an article about the people behind.

BERNARD DARWIN

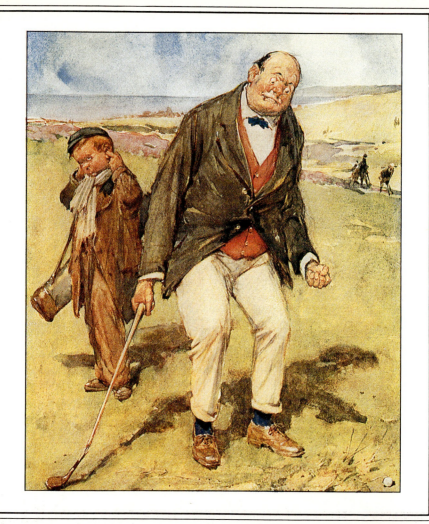

from
OFF MY GAME

"I'm off my game," the golfer said,
  And shook his locks in woe;
"My putter never lays me dead,
  My drives will never go;
Howe'er I swing, howe'er I stand,
  Results are still the same,
I'm in the burn, I'm in the sand —
  I'm off my game!

"Oh, would that such mishaps might fall
  On Laidlay or Macfie,
That they might toe or heel the ball,
  And sclaff along like me!
Men hurry from me in the street,
  And execrate my name,
Old partners shun me when we meet —
  I'm off my game!

"I hate the sight of all my set,
  I grow morose as Byron;
I never loved a brassey yet,
  And now I hate an iron.
My cleek seems merely made to top,
  My putting's wild or tame;
It's really time for me to stop —
  I'm off my game!"

ANDREW LANG

from
THE GOLFIAD

Arma virumque cano. — Virgil, *Æn.* i. l. 1

BALLS, clubs, and men I sing, who first, methinks,
Made sport and bustle on North Berwick Links,
Brought coin and fashion, betting, and renown,
Champagne and claret, to a country town,
And lords and ladies, knights and squires to ground
Where washerwomen erst and snobs were found!

The game is ancient — manly — and employs,
In its departments, women, men, and boys:
Men play the game, the boys the clubs convey,
And lovely woman gives the prize away,
When August brings the great, the medal day!
Nay, more: tho' some may doubt, and sneer, and scoff,
The female muse has sung the game of Golf,
And trac'd it down, with choicest skill and grace,
Thro' all its bearings, to the human race;
The tee, the start of youth — the game, our life —
The ball when fairly bunkered, man and wife.
GEORGE FULLERTON CARNEGIE

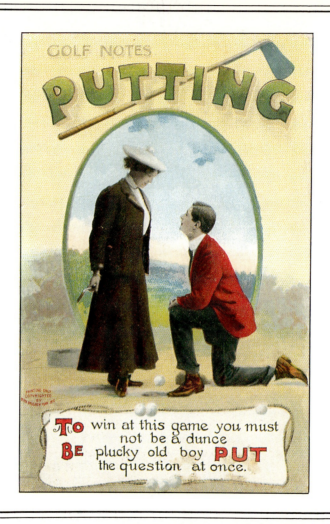

LOVE'S HAZARD

On the links I first admired you,
  Rivals all with ease defeating;
In your golfing red attired, you
  Looked divine, my pretty sweeting!
Then and there I straight aspired to
  Win your hand with amorous greeting;
Luck and Cupid both conspired to
  Bring me bliss that "Summer Meeting."

But three months, alas! have flown by;
  Now I see my hopes were fleeting;
And this fact you've clearly shown by
  Scornfully my homage treating.
For about the links alone I
  Must behold — my woe completing —
You and *him*, and thus bemoan I
  Such a sorry "Autumn Meeting!"
                        L. C. H. G.

THE GOLFING GHOST

His name had not been mentioned
   Among the list of blest,
Who from things mathematical
   Had found eternal rest:
His second time attempted,
   But ploughed — I think they say —
Yes! ploughed by cruel Examiners,
   Close to St. Andrews Bay.

Oh how the perspiration
   Of grief began to pour,
As taking up his driver
   He turned towards the shore.
One look around the College —
   He could not go astray —
For he saw the white foam dashing
   In wild St. Andrews Bay.

Down to the Links he hurried,
   His brow was sad and low:
Already — it was pale moonlight —
   He heard the tempest blow:
His gown was on his shoulders —
   A scarlet gown, they say —
As he faced the raging waters
   Of old St. Andrews Bay.

He drove from off the teeing-ground
   A never-falling ball:
Then rushed among the surges,
   They were a fitting pall!
A corpse was found next morning
   Floating far, far away,
Far from the stormy billows
   Of wild St. Andrews Bay.

There are who tell the story,
   Some Caddies by the shore,
How on some wintry evenings,
   When ocean tempests roar,
A figure white's seen golfing
   Golfing, not far away,
White as the foaming billows
   Of old St. Andrews Bay.
                    R. Barclay

from
THE HEART OF A GOOF

IT WAS A morning when all nature shouted "Fore!" The breeze, as it blew gently up from the valley, seemed to bring a message of hope and cheer, whispering of chip-shots holed and brassies landing squarely on the meat. The fairway, as yet unscarred by the irons of a hundred dubs, smiled greenly up at the azure sky; and the sun, peeping above the trees, looked like a giant golf-ball perfectly lofted by the mashie of some unseen god and about to drop dead by the pin of the eighteenth. It was the day of the opening of the course after the long winter, and a crowd of considerable dimensions had collected at the first tee. Plus fours gleamed in the sunshine, and the air was charged with happy anticipation.

P. G. WODEHOUSE

from
THE WOODEN PUTTER

IF YOU WISH a good putter of wood you will hardly expect to find one in a club-maker's ready-made stock, far less in a toyshop or a tobacconist's window. The putter must be sought for with care and not hastily, for she is to be the friend, be it hoped, of many years. First then find out a workman of repute as a maker of putters — and in these days of "reach me down" clubs there are few such artists — and having found him proceed warily. It will never do to go and order him to make you a first-class club for your match next morning; you would probably receive only the work of an apprentice. Wait your time and you will find the great man about his shop or on his doorstep at the dinner hour.

If a half-empty pipe lies beside him offer him a cigar, and mention that you are afraid that it is not as good as you would have wished, being the last of the box, at the same time giving him to understand that another box is expected that evening. The cigar having been accepted and lighted, you may, in the course of conversation, allude to a very fine putter made by a rival clubmaker which, you will tell your friend, is being much talked about and copied. This will be almost certainly a winning card to play, for there is much jealousy among the profession, and as likely as not the remark will be made that So-and-so — naming the rival maker — has about as much idea of fashioning a putter as he has of successfully solving the problem of aerial navigation.

Do not press the matter to a conclusion, but meet your man again in a similar manner, this time carelessly holding in your hand the club which you have long felt was the cause of the success of some distinguished player. Almost seem to hide it from the clubmaker, and he will be sure to ask to see it, and probably volunteer to make you one on the same lines with slight improvements of his own. In time you will get your putter, and it will probably be a good one.

JOHN L. LOW

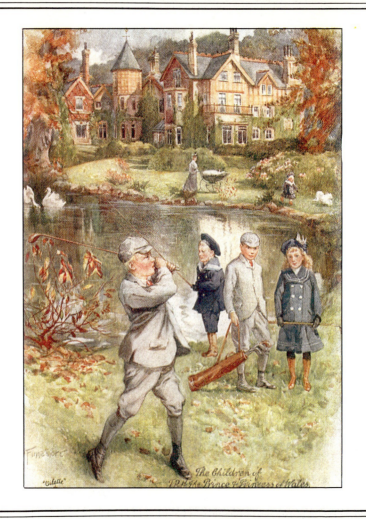

"Tatette" The Children of T.R.H. the Prince & Princess of Wales

from
THE MORNING ROUND (6-8 A.M.)

BEAUTIFUL ROUND! superbly played —
Round where never mistake is made;
Who with enchantment would not bound
For the Round of the Morning, Beautiful Round?

Never a duffer is out of bed;
None but the choicest of bricks instead
On the links, at *six*, can ever be found;
Round of the Morning, Beautiful Round!

There they lie in a hideous doze
Different quite from a golfer's repose —
That from which he starts with a bound
For the Round of the Morning, Beautiful Round!

Agile and light, each tendon strung,
With healthy play of each active lung,
He strides along o'er the dewy ground
In the Round of the Morning, Beautiful Round!

Beautiful Round! most cleverly won
Under the gaze of the rising sun,
And hailed with a pleasant chuckling sound;
Round of the Morning, Beautiful Round!

Beautiful Round! I think of thee
Through months of labour and misery:—
Round thee the strings of my heart are wound,
Round of the Morning, Beautiful Round!

"THE GLUTTON."

from
THE GOLFER AT HOME

THE GOLFER, having finished a large and late breakfast, lights a cigar, and turns his steps towards the links and the club; so far there is nothing unusual in his proceedings. Presently he is joined by another, and then another golfer, and about eleven o'clock little knots form in front of the club and in the parlour, and the process of match-making begins. There is only one thing more difficult than getting a good match, and that is, avoiding a bad one. A man must be firm, and sometimes slightly unscrupulous, if he would be spared a match which will make him miserable for the day; for if he once begins a match he is bound in honour to play it all day, and he cannot better his condition. It is therefore a necessary though painful duty to himself always to be engaged till he falls in with a match which he thinks he can play with comfort and amusement. The most handsome and gentlemanly apologies from a bad partner afford no reparation for a lost day. It is of no use his trying to beguile the time, and soothe your wounded feelings by pleasant remarks and occasional jokes, if you are obliged to spend the day with your heavy iron in your hand, to enable you to dig him out of every sand-hole he puts his and your ball into. It is no substantial consolation to abuse him and his play heartily, as of course you will do, whenever you escape from him. The day has been lost, and probably both temper and money too. Be warned in time, and never, except in peculiar circumstances, be so entrapped. This may seem hard advice, but no one knows till he tries what a painful thing an unequal and uncongenial alliance in golf, as in matrimony, is.

H. J. M.

DUFFERS YET

A Parody
By Two "Long Spoons"

After years of play together,
After fair and stormy weather,
After rounds of every green,
From Westward Ho to Aberdeen —
Why did e'er we buy a set,
If we must be duffers yet?
          Duffers yet! Duffers yet!

After singles, foursomes — all,
Fractured club and cloven ball;
After grief in sand and whin,
Foozled drives, and "putts" not in —
Ev'n our caddies scarce regret,
When we part as duffers yet.
          Duffers yet! Duffers yet!

Must it ever then be thus?
Failure most mysterious!
Shall we never fairly stand,
Eye on ball as club in hand?
Are the bounds eternal set
To retain us duffers yet?
          Duffers yet! Duffers yet!
              M. T. S. D.

SEASIDE GOLF

How straight it flew, how long it flew,
   It clear'd the rutty track
And soaring, disappeared from view
   Beyond the bunker's back —
A glorious, sailing, bounding drive
That made me glad I was alive.

And down the fairway, far along
   It glowed a lonely white;
I played an iron sure and strong
   And clipp'd it out of sight,
And spite of grassy banks between
I knew I'd find it on the green.

And so I did. It lay content
   Two paces from the pin;
A steady putt and then it went
   Oh, most securely in.
The very turf rejoiced to see
That quite unprecedented three.

Ah! seaweed smells from sandy caves
   And thyme and mist in whiffs,
In-coming tide, Atlantic waves
   Slapping the sunny cliffs,
Lark song and sea sounds in the air
And splendour, splendour everywhere.

                    Sir John Betjeman

IN PRAISE OF GOLF

She that golf hath never tried,
Nor made "Badminton" her guide,
Knows not the enthralling might
Of that pastime of delight.

What are honours, regal wealth,
Florid youth, and rosy health,
Without golf its pleasure brings?—
Impotent, unmeaning things!

Gentle ladies, persevere,
Still, in scoring be sincere;
Pros. and practice soon will do
Much, if hand and eye be true.
L. C. H. G.

from
HIGH STAKES

IT HAS BEEN well said — I think by the man who wrote the subtitles for "Cage-Birds of Society" (began the Oldest Member) — that wealth does not always bring happiness. It was so with Bradbury Fisher, the hero of the story which I am about to relate. One of America's most prominent tainted millionaires, he had two sorrows in life — his handicap refused to stir from twenty-four and his wife disapproved of his collection of famous golf relics. Once, finding him crooning over the trousers in which Ouimet had won his historic replay against Vardon and Ray in the American Open, she had asked him why he did not collect something worth while, like Old Masters or first editions.

Worth while! Bradbury had forgiven, for he loved the woman, but he could not forget.

For Bradbury Fisher, like so many men who have taken to the game in middle age, after a youth misspent in the pursuits of commerce, was no half-hearted enthusiast. Although he still occasionally descended on Wall Street in order to pry the small investor loose from another couple of million, what he really lived for now was golf and his collection. He had begun the collection in his first year as a golfer, and he prized it dearly. And when he reflected that his wife had stopped him purchasing J. H. Taylor's shirt-stud, which he could have had for a few hundred pounds, the iron seemed to enter into his soul.

P. G. WODEHOUSE

from
A ROUND WITH THE PRO.

(1) If any perfection
    Exists on this earth
Immune from correction,
    Unmeet for our mirth,

(2) The despair of the scoffer,
    The doom of the wit,
A professional golfer,
    I fancy, is it.

(3) No faults and no vices
    Are found in this man,
He pulls not nor slices,
    It don't seem he can;

(4) Like an angel from heaven,
    With grief, not with blame,
He points out the seven
    Worst faults in your game.

(5) "You should hold your club this way."
    He tells you, "not *that*."
You hold your club his way —
    It hurts you, my hat!

(6) Your hocks and your haunches,
    Your hands and your hips
He assembles and launches
    On unforeseen trips.

(7) He says you should do it
    Like *so* and like *so*;
Your legs become suet,
    Your limbs are as dough.

(8) You mark his beginning,
    You watch how he ends,
You observe the ball spinning,
    How high it ascends!

(9) He tells you the divot
    You took with your last
Was all due to the pivot —
    Your comment is "Blast!".

(10) He tells you your shoulders
    Don't sink as they should;
Your intellect moulders,
    Your brains are like wood.

(11) But *he* pulls his wrists through
   Right under his hands,
His whole body twists through;
   Tremendous he stands.

(12) He stands there and whops them
   Without any fuss;
He scoops not nor tops them
   Because he goes *thus*.

(13) Obsequious batches
   Of dutiful spheres
All day he despatches
   Through Time and the years.

(14) You copy his motions,
   You take it like *this*,
You seize all his notions,
   You strike — and you miss.

(15) You aim with persistence,
   With verve and with flair,
You gaze at the distance —
   The orb is not there.

(16) The hands have been lifted,
   The head remains still,
Your eyes have not shifted —
   No, nor has the pill.

(17) He points out the errors
   He told you before,
To add to your terrors
   He points out two more.

(18) Till, your eyes growing glassy,
   Your face like a mule's,
You let out with your brassie
   Regardless of rules.

(19) And the ball goes careering
   Far into the sky
And is seen disappearing
   Due south, over Rye.

(20) You stand staring wildly
   (It's now at Madrid)
And the pro. remarks mildly,
   "You see what you did?

(21) You made every movement
   I've tried to explain;
That shows great improvement,
   Now do it again."

EVOE

THE DREADFUL HOLLOW

I HATE the dreadful hollow beyond the seventh hole;
  All day in the sand below the niblicks hurtle and flash;
The tortured air is hot with the breathings of some lost soul;
  And the breezes there, whenever they blow from it, whisper — "Dash!"

                              E. M. GRIFFITHS

from
AFTER TEA

THERE IS THAT about golf after tea, even if we do not play a game, but only chip about with a mashie, which is of a scrumptious and heavenly quality — so heavenly indeed that, whether or not it is very selfish of me, I like to play it best by myself. In fact, I have just come this moment from doing so. I had the field to myself. There is a horse that lives in this field. He is a thoroughly amiable horse, but of rather too friendly and inquisitive a nature, and comes prancing at me so sociably as to disturb the perfect concentration. On this blessed occasion he had been put to bed early; I caught a glimpse of him looking wistfully out of his stall, I knew that all was well and so to slogging.

That last is not a good golfing word, but it is used deliberately. There is a delicious temptation to hit hard after tea, because at that time the stiffest of us feel comparatively lithe and lissom. It seems easier to cultivate that beautiful, impalpable little pause at the top of the swing, to wait and gather ourselves together and bang the ball with an internal cry of: "This shall not go for naething." To-morrow morning we shall be as stiff as ever again and stiffer, the gift of timing will have gone as utterly as has the sunset, but after tea we can still have our "moments of glad grace." Whether the ball really goes farther than it does earlier in the day I am not prepared to say on oath. At any rate we think it does, and that, when we are by ourselves, is all that matters. The enchantment of the hour lends distance to the shot, and the darker it gets the farther the ball appears to go. It is a mistake to become so enthusiastic as to measure the shot, for that, step we never so short, is a disillusioning process. In this field I know my distances pretty well, but I never let myself remember them after tea; and so home, flushed, elated, " and in my heart some late lark singing"; my goodness! how those shots did go.

BERNARD DARWIN

"FAR AND SURE!"

"Far and Sure!" 'twas the cry of our fathers,
   'Twas a cry which their forefathers heard;
'Tis the cry of their sons when the mustering gathers:
   When we're gone may it still be the word:

"Far and Sure!" there is honour and hope in the sound;
   Long over these Links may it roll!
It will — O it will! for each face around
   Shows its magic is felt in each soul.

Let it guide us in life; at the desk or the bar,
   It will shield us from folly's gay lure;
Then tho' rough be the course, and the winning-post *far*,
   We will carry the stakes — O be *sure!*

Let it guide us in Golf, whether "Burgess" or "Star";
   At the last round let none look demure!
All Golfers are brothers when *driving* is *far*,
   When putting is canny and *sure.*

"Far and Sure! Far and Sure!" fill the bumper and drain it,
   May our motto for ever endure;
May time never maim it, nor dishonour stain it,
   Then drink, brothers, a drink, "Far and Sure!"

By the late Sheriff Logan.

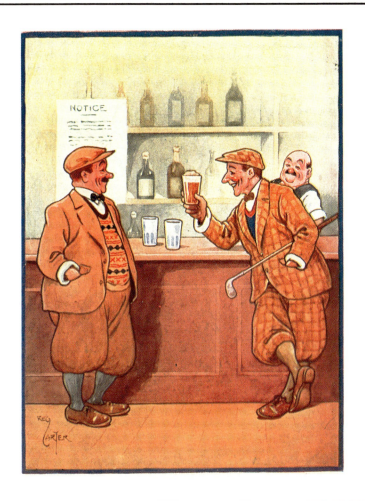

Acknowledgements

I must first thank Ms Jennie Davies of Michael Joseph and Mr David White of Golfiana Miscellania and Mr W. Ransome for a great deal of help and encouragement.

The editor and publishers wish to thank *The Times* for permission to quote the extracts on pages 13 and 45 and A.P. Watt & Son for those on pages 25 and 39. Permission to quote the poem on page 35 was granted by John Murray and that on page 40 by the proprietors of *Punch*.

The illustrations on pages 6, 14, 16, 20, 27, 28, 31, 32, 38, 41, 44, 47 and 48 appear by courtesy of Golfiana Miscellania; and those on pages 3, 4, 5, 8, 19, 22, 25, 34, 37 and 43 were supplied by the Mary Evans Picture Library.

I have been unable to trace the owners of certain copyrights and beg the forgiveness of anyone whose rights have been overlooked.